Blue Mountain Arts®

Bestselling Books

By Susan Polis Schutz:
To My Daughter, with Love, on the Important Things in Life
To My Son, with Love
I Love You

100 Things to Always Remember… and One Thing to Never Forget
by Alin Austin

Is It Time to Make a Change?
by Deanna Beisser

Trust in Yourself
by Donna Fargo

To the One Person I Consider to Be My Soul Mate
by D. Pagels

For You, Just Because You're Very Special to Me
by Collin McCarty

Chasing Away the Clouds
by Douglas Pagels

A Lifetime of Love …Poems on the Passages of Life
by Leonard Nimoy

Anthologies:
42 Gifts I'd Like to Give to You
Always Believe in Yourself and Your Dreams
Creeds of Life, Love, & Inspiration
Don't Ever Give Up Your Dreams
Follow Your Dreams Wherever They Lead You
For You, My Daughter
Friends Are Forever
Friends for Life
I Love You, Mom
I'm Glad You Are My Sister
The Joys and Challenges of Motherhood
The Language of Recovery …and Living Life One Day at a Time
Life Can Be Hard Sometimes …but It's Going to Be Okay
Marriage Is a Promise of Love
May You Always Have an Angel by Your Side
Mottos to Live By
Teaching and Learning Are Lifelong Journeys
There Is Greatness Within You, My Son
These Are the Gifts I'd Like to Give to You
Think Positive Thoughts Every Day
Thoughts of Friendship
Thoughts to Share with a Wonderful Teenager
To My Child
True Friends Always Remain in Each Other's Heart
With God by Your Side …You Never Have to Be Alone

Take Each Day One Step at a Time

Poems to Inspire
and Encourage
the Journey to Recovery

A Special Updated
Blue Mountain Arts® Collection

Blue Mountain Press™

SPS Studios, Inc., Boulder, Colorado

Library of Congress Catalog Card Number: 94-34185
ISBN: 0-88396-641-7 (hardcover)
ISBN: 0-88396-395-7 (trade paper)

ACKNOWLEDGMENTS appear on page 64.

Certain trademarks are used under license.

Manufactured in China
First printing of this edition: June 2002

♻ *This book is printed on recycled paper.*

This book is printed on fine quality, laid embossed, 80 lb. paper. This paper has been specially produced to be acid free (neutral pH) and contains no groundwood or unbleached pulp. It conforms with all the requirements of the American National Standards Institute, Inc., so as to ensure that this book will last and be enjoyed by future generations.

Library of Congress Cataloging-in-Publication Data

Take each day one step at a time : a Blue Mountain Arts collection.
       p. cm.
   ISBN 0-88396-641-7 (hardcover: alk. paper)
   ISBN 0-88396-395-7 (trade paper: alk. paper)
   1. Self-actualization (Psychology)—Poetry. 2. American poetry—20th century. I.
SPS Studios (Firm)
   PS595.S45T35 1994
   811'.008-dc20

                                                    94-34185
                                                    CIP

SPS Studios, Inc.
P.O. Box 4549, Boulder, Colorado 80306

Contents

Take Each Day
One Step at a Time

Remember... there is a deeper strength
and an amazing abundance of peace
available to you.
Draw from this well;
call on your faith to uphold you.
You will make it through this time
and find joy in life again.

Life continues around us,
even when our troubles seem to stop time.
There is good in life every day.
Take a few minutes to distract yourself
from your concerns —
long enough to draw strength from a tree
or to find pleasure in a bird's song.
Return a smile;
realize that life is a series of levels,
cycles of ups and downs —
some easy, some challenging.
Through it all, we learn;
we grow strong in faith;
we mature in understanding.
The difficult times are often
the best teachers, and there is
good to be found in all situations.
Reach for the good.
Be strong, and don't give up.

— Pamela Owens Renfro

In the
Difficult Times,
Keep Believing in Yourself

There are times in life
when things are not perfect,
when problems seem to surround you.
As you look for a way through them,
it's important to keep
a positive attitude about your life
and where you are going.
You may wonder if you're making
the right choices.
You may wonder about how things
will turn out
if you take a different road.
But you are a strong
and motivated individual
who will rise to meet
the challenges that face you.
You are a loving and warm person
who loves life,
and you will get through
the difficult times.

— Beverly A. Chisley

In time, you will smile again
    and truly feel it,
and your laughter will be genuine.
But until your pain has gone away,
and your sadness has disappeared,
    don't feel you have to be strong.
What you're feeling is real.
Don't feel like you're wrong
    if you want to cry.

There are some roads in life
that we must travel alone,
even though we may be
surrounded by people whom we love.
Some things in life,
    such as what you're feeling now,
can't be felt by anyone but you.

But just remember
you are not alone at all;
everyone who loves you
is walking with you in spirit,
and will be there with you.
You'll find a new strength,
a new peace, and a new happiness.
It just takes a little time.

— Laurie Wymer

"Words of Wisdom"

Sometimes the paths we take are long and hard, but remember: those are always the ones that lead to the most beautiful views ❧ Challenges come along, inevitably; how you respond to them determines who you are — deep down inside — and everything you're going to be ❧ Increase the chances of reaching your goals by working at them gradually ❧ The very best you can do is all that is asked of you ❧ Realize that you are capable of working miracles of your own making ❧ Remember that it's up to you to find the key that unlocks the door to a more fulfilling life ❧ Understand that increased difficulty brings you nearer to the truth of how to survive it — and get beyond it ❧ Cross your bridges ❧ Meet your challenges ❧ Reach out for your dreams, and bring them closer and closer to your heart ❧ Get rid of the "if only's," and get on with whatever you need to do to get things right in your life ❧

— Collin McCarty

This Can Be a
Time of Growth

As difficult as this time in your life
*   may be,*
you will become stronger if you
face each day with patience and hope;
if you accept your weaknesses
but concentrate on your strengths;
if you love and care for yourself
even when you are angry and confused;
if you can look at doubt and fear
but keep your mind on the fact that
the struggle is helping you to grow
*   in faith and confidence.*
If you gently
pick yourself up when you fall
and continue walking;
if you keep thinking about
all the things you can do well,
all the things that bring you joy,
and all the people you love
*   who also love you;*
if you hold on to your goals
even though the way to reach them
*   may be unclear, then...*

You can see the troubling times
almost as friends who have come
to help you grow further
than you thought you could;
friends who are showing you the way
to a more courageous heart;
friends who help you to see that
you are more powerful than
you ever thought you were;
friends who help you to see that
the hard times are making you more open
to accepting life as it comes,
and realizing that you have
the inner strength and loving nature
to deal successfully with
any difficult moment.

— *Donna Levine Small*

The First Step You Take
Is Always
the Most Important One

The first few steps you take
on any journey
won't get you where you want to go.
But without those first steps
and the many more that follow,
you would always be standing
right where you are,
looking towards the future
and wondering what it would
really be like
to see your world
the way you always
dreamed it could be.

One of the greatest lessons
in life is the one you learn
about moving forward
and taking steps to reach your goals.
Life rewards those who are willing
to be involved in it
and take chances.
Take your chance
and take those first few steps,
because a better life is just waiting
for you.

— Nick Santana

You are beginning a personal journey.
At times you may expect the answers to
come quickly, but try to be patient;
some answers may take a lifetime to be
revealed to you.

Though you may be a little uncertain now
and your confidence may be shaken,
you will stand on your own feet soon enough.
Your legs will grow to be strong under you;
they will take you where you want to go.

You'll make mistakes along the way;
a fork in the road may present a path that
you later decide was the wrong way to go.
Take the time to learn from your mistakes,
but don't be too hard on yourself.

You are learning to make your own choices,
and there is great joy in that.
You are a human being who is embarking
on the important journey of discovering
who you are and what you have to offer.
Celebrate your uniqueness, and you will
triumph on your life's journey.

— Deborah Weinberg

You will be whatever you resolve to be. Determine to be something in the world, and you will be something.

"I cannot," never accomplished anything.

But "I will try," has worked wonders.

— Joel Hawes

Peace and Happiness
Must Come from Within

Whatever a person becomes
on the outside
must first be believed
in the heart.
We all become different people
as we grow older,
with different hopes and dreams,
goals and achievements,
memories and feelings.
No one can ever say that, as a person,
they are all they can be,
for it is then that they
have stopped growing from within.

In a time of new beginnings,
continue to grow, to dream,
and to make new memories.
Whatever gives you peace
within yourself
will allow others to see
the special person you truly are.

— Shirley Vander Pol

When You Need Some Help to Get Through the Day...

When nothing is going right.
When you're wondering, "What
   did I do to deserve this?"
When the day is a disaster,
and a little serenity
   is just what you're after.
When you need a whole lot less
   to concern you,
and a whole lot more to smile about.
When a few peaceful hours
   would seem like a vacation to you,
and you're wondering if there's anything
   you've got to look forward to...
Sometimes you just have to remember:
   It _really_ _is_ going to be okay.
   You're going to make it
      through this day.
   Even if it's one step at a time.
Sometimes you just have to be
   patient and brave and strong.
If you don't know how, just
   make it up as you go along.
And hold on to your hope as though it
   were a path to follow
      or a song you love to sing.
Because if you have hope,
   you have everything.

— Collin McCarty

Hope is not the closing of your eyes
   to the difficulty, the risk,
   or the failure.

It is a trust that —
   if I fail now —
   I shall not fail forever;
   and if I am hurt,
      I shall be healed.

It is a trust that
   life is good,
   love is powerful,
   and the future is full of promise.

                              — Anonymous

Recovery Is a Learning Process

Recovery is about learning to love and value yourself enough to stop destroying yourself. It's about learning to change your mind and your heart. It's about forgiving yourself and others. It's about letting go of shame and learning to accept your true self.

Recovery is about letting go of the lofty expectation of perfection that you have placed upon yourself and others. It's learning to love and accept yourself and others unconditionally.

Recovery is about learning to use your anger as the fuel to create something good, rather than denying it or holding it inside until you self-destruct or strike out at another.

Recovery is about learning that you have a choice: You can choose to be hopeful rather than hopeless; you can choose to act from faith rather than react from fear; and you can choose to enjoy life rather than merely survive it.

— Donna Newman

Don't Be Afraid to
Talk About What You're Feeling

Good or bad, feelings need expression;
they must be recognized and given
freedom to reveal themselves.
It isn't wise to hide behind a smile
when your heart is breaking;
that is not being true to how
you feel inside.
By letting out your feelings,
your pain is released,
and you are able to go on —
to reconstruct your life and
think of other things
that will make you happy again.

Put away the myth that says
you must be strong enough to face
the whole world with a smile and
a brave attitude all of the time.
You have your feelings that say otherwise,
so admit that they are there.
Use their healing power
to put the past behind you,
and realize those expressive
stirrings in your heart
are very much a part of you.
Use them to get better,
to find peace within,
to be true to yourself.

— Barbara J. Hall

*Sometimes admitting our weaknesses
is the bravest thing we can do,
because with that admission,
we drop our shield of pretense,
find the courage to face reality,
and reach out for the help we need.*

    *It is said that the first step
on the road to recovery
is the hardest.
But while the road
is not always an easy one,
recovery offers you a new chance
to learn to love yourself,
your family, and life.
It takes time to get adjusted
to a new way of living
and to learn to enjoy
the peacefulness that recovery offers.
There will be times
when you will feel anxious,
and that's normal.
But you deserve to live in love
and happiness,
and there is no greater gift
you could give yourself.*

                       — *Donna Newman*

The Serenity Prayer

God grant me the serenity
to accept the things
   I cannot change;
the courage to change
   the things I can;
and the wisdom
   to know the difference.

— Reinhold Niebuhr

The Ghosts in Our Lives

Our lives are filled with ghosts
Skeleton ties
To people we have loved
Their shadows reappear
When memory breathes life into them
Shades of our parents
Impressions of old lovers
We paint anew
On the faces of strangers and friends
That enter our lives
Our ghosts
They visit us again and again
Until we learn
What they have come to teach us
And we master the puzzle that
We are partners in
We wrestle with our ghosts
Until we put them to sleep
Silence them
By listening to them at last

— Parvene Michaels

Detachment

We are all attached
in some way
to the baggage of the past or the
desires of our hearts and minds for tomorrow.

The umbilical cords that connect each of us
to these empty and artificial times
grow thicker with every passing
day and subsequent event.

We must all learn to detach from
the demands and pulls of the unknown
and our concern for the past.

To detach
is to let go, not of the thing
but of the need for the thing.

To detach
is to let go of the dependency on a person
but to hold on to the preference
for the person.

To detach
is to let go of the habit, not the
desire for the pleasure of the outcome.

To detach
is to release the old you
and embrace the new you.

— Tim Connor

Autobiography in Five Short Chapters
by Portia Nelson

Chapter I

I walk down the street.
There is a deep hole in the sidewalk.
I fall in.
I am lost... I am helpless.
It isn't my fault.
It takes forever to find a way out.

Chapter II

I walk down the same street.
There is a deep hole in the sidewalk.
*I **pretend** I don't see it.*
I fall in again.
I can't believe I am in this same place.
But, it isn't my fault.
It still takes a long time to get out.

Chapter III

I walk down the same street.
There is a deep hole in the sidewalk.
*I **see** it there.*
I still fall in... it's a habit... but,
my eyes are open.
I know where I am.
*It is **my** fault.*
I get out immediately.

Chapter IV

I walk down the same street.
There is a deep hole in the sidewalk.
I walk around it.

Chapter V

I walk down another street.

Peace Is Coming

Rest assured
    that peace is at hand.
    The time is coming
    when all of your
    self-built walls
    and guarded halls
    will wither to dust.

The free-flowing love
    of your spirit within
    soon will be released
        to love
    and, as it has been your
        desire from birth,
    to find a spirit
    who will not chain you
        or claim you
        as a possession,
    who will not crush
        your inner being
    as a flower is crushed
    by an unfaithful hand.

Rest assured
    that the time is coming
    for you simply
        to share,
        to grow,
        to learn,
        to love.
                — L. Dale Cox

I'm Finally Learning to Just Be "Me," and It Feels Wonderful

Ever since I can remember,
I've been a codependent person.
I always tried my hardest
to please other people.
When it came to others' feelings,
I would put them before my own —
even if it meant
sacrificing my own needs.
I cared too much about
what others thought of me.
I tried to be everyone's friend.
I was a "people pleaser":
doing, saying, and being
whatever everyone else
wanted me to be.
I lost out on knowing who I really was.
It reached the point where
I didn't even know what I wanted in life.
I was unable
to make even simple decisions,
because in a way,
I had lost my true identity.

I'm still a codependent person —
but now I'm a recovering one.
I recognize my weaknesses,
and because I can now put myself first —
before everyone else —
I can finally be "me."

— Sherée Heller

"My Focus Is on Wellness"
...An Affirmation for
Healing and Recovery

Each day, each minute, is
no longer a struggle.
Somehow, my body is now free.
I can sit in silence and focus
on my breathing.
I am no longer distracted.
My body is now working
for me, not against me.

My mind is now experiencing
a serenity I have never known before.
I have developed an inner strength
that carries me through
even the most difficult times.
I can now focus on my goals
and desires.

Every experience of my life
is somehow new again.
My senses are more acute
than ever before.
I find pleasure in every task,
no matter how routine it is.

There is a place of healing
inside me now
where I feel as if I am standing
on a beach covered with
    crystal-white sand,
surrounded by sparkling blue water.
I feel the sand between my toes
and the sun beaming down my back.
I stand near the water
and the tides seem
    to reach towards me,
but I am now flowing with the currents
and not against them.

— *Marcy Perlmutter*

Be Hopeful... Think Positive

Learn to accept... what the past has given,
what the present is,
and all that life has to bring.
Remind yourself of the important things...
and where your heart is heading!
Have Confidence...
Be Motivated...
and fill the air with your laughter.
Remember your Guardian Angel
who stands just a whisper away.
Explore the goodness of your soul,
and use the tools from within.
Be Hopeful...
Think Positive...
and allow your heart to be happy.

Retain the knowledge of knowing
that Faith can move mountains.
Permit your heart to believe
beyond yesterday's belief.
Be Strong...
Stay Focused...
and grant your soul permission to dance.
Keep in mind... the power of prayer
and the mysteries of Heaven.
Get in tune with your intuition
and be determined to trust Divine Providence.
Have Courage...
Persevere...
and kiss life... with your smile!

— Michele Rossi

A New Strength

There are times in every life
when we feel hurt or alone...
But I believe that these times
when we feel lost
and all around us seems
    to be falling apart
    are really bridges of growth.
We struggle and try to recapture
    the security of what was,
    but almost in spite of ourselves,
    we emerge on the other side
    with a new understanding,
      a new awareness,
      a new strength.
It is almost as though
    we must go through the pain
    and the struggle
      in order to grow
and reach new heights.

— Sue Mitchell

Be True to Yourself,
No Matter What

Right now, you are struggling
  with your inner world.
You are asking yourself
  how you feel about everything
and if you are really happy.
You are changing into
  the exact person
that you were hoping to become,
but now you find that these changes
  are causing difficulties
for the people around you.
They want you to remain
  the same person that you've been;
they may even want you to be
  something for them
rather than being yourself.
But now is the time to make
  a statement about your life.
You must continue to follow
  your own chosen path
and make alterations in
  your lifestyle.

You will find your new place
  in the circle of your loved ones,
but keep in mind that
everyone must create their own
  sense of self and happiness.
No one should be shaped or confined
by someone else's ideals of
  what they should be.
Strive for your own beliefs
  and desires;
continue to make your world complete
by being yourself.
Every day, discover something
  new and unique about yourself,
and remember that happiness
  and contentment in life
come when you focus on
  your own goals,
being yourself, and making the most of
every minute of your life.

— *Dena Dilaconi*

Beginning Today...

Today
look in a mirror
and notice
that the person
who greets you
is beautiful,
inside and out.

Today
say to yourself that
you know nothing is
impossible.
Remind yourself that
every one of your dreams
is within reach.

Today
think about all of
the people who love you,
who see the beauty in you,
and begin to look at yourself
in the same way.

— Lise Schlosser

Learn to Let Go...

If you want to be healthy morally, mentally and physically, just let go. Let go of the little annoyances of everyday life, the irritations and the petty vexations that cross your path daily. Don't take them up, nurse them, pet them, and brood over them. They are not worthwhile. Let them go!

Learn to let go. As you value health of body and peace of mind, let go — just simply let go!

— Anonymous

Finish every day and be done with it. You have done what you could. Some blunders and absurdities no doubt crept in; forget them as soon as you can. Tomorrow is a new day; begin it well and serenely, and with too high a spirit to be cumbered with your old nonsense. This day is all that is good and fair. It is too dear, with its hopes and invitations, to waste a moment on the yesterdays.

— Ralph Waldo Emerson

Have Faith...

Faith begins
by believing
in your heart
that what is right
has a chance.

It is knowing
in your heart
that good can
overcome evil,
that the sun can shine
after a rainstorm.

Faith is peaceful
and comforting;
it comes from within
where no one
can invade
your private dreams.

Faith is not something
you can demand or command;
it is a commitment
to a belief.

Faith is believing
in something that
you cannot see or hear,
something deep inside
that only you understand
and control.

Faith is trusting
in yourself
enough to know
that no matter
how things turn out,
you will make
the best of them.

— Beth Fagan Quinn

May You Find Serenity

May you find serenity and tranquility in a world
you may not always understand. May the pain
you have known and the conflict you have
experienced give you the strength to walk through
life facing each new situation with courage and
optimism. Always know that there are those
whose love and understanding will always be
there, even when you feel most alone. May a kind
word, a reassuring touch, and a warm smile be
yours every day of your life, and may you give
these gifts as well as receive them. Realize that
what you may feel you lack in one regard may be
more than compensated for in another. What you
feel you lack in the present may become one of
your strengths in the future. May you see your
future as one filled with promise and possibility.
Learn to view everything as a worthwhile
experience. May you find enough inner strength
to determine your own worth by yourself, and
not be dependent on another's judgment of your
accomplishments. May you always feel loved.

— Sandra Sturtz Hauss

What You Are Doing
Takes Real Courage

Courage is the feeling that you can make it,
no matter how challenging the situation.
It is knowing that you can reach out
for help and you are not alone.
Courage is accepting each day,
knowing that you have the inner resources
to deal with the ordinary things
as well as the confusing things,
with the exciting things
as well as the painful things.
Courage is taking the time
to get involved with life, family,
and friends,
and giving your love and energy
in whatever ways you can.

Courage is being who you are,
being aware of your good qualities
and talents,
and not worrying about
what you do not have.
Courage is allowing yourself to live
as fully as you can,
to experience as much of life
as you are able to,
to grow and develop yourself
in whatever directions you need to.
Courage is having hope for the future
and trust in the natural flow of life.
It is being open to change.
Courage is having faith that life
is a beautiful gift.

— Donna Levine Small

Someone Is Always There for You

Stressful situations and trying times
are some of the realities of life.
When you experience them,
you may think they'll never leave.
But even the most difficult times come and go,
and the strength you need to meet
the situation
will be there for you in the helping hand
of a friend,
in the compassion of a loved one
who cares,
and in the listening ear of someone who knows
what you're going through.
All you have to do is look up and reach out,
and someone will be there
to share your troubles.

— Linda E. Knight

Be Kind to Yourself...

There will always be times
when it's hard to remember
your strengths.
These are the times
when you need
to give yourself special attention.
Be kind to yourself...
Kindness nurtures
and gives hope
to growing dreams.
Respect yourself...
Listen to your needs,
and treat yourself
as you would a friend.
Encourage yourself...
Remember what you truly want,
and fight for it
as you would your life.
Appreciate yourself...
Don't take for granted
the qualities
that make you unique.
Focus yourself...
It is with discipline
and motivation
that you will move towards your goals.
Be giving towards yourself...
In that way, your strength will thrive,
and you'll be realizing your goals
a day at a time.

— Gail Mutterperl

Only You Know What Is Best for You

You cannot listen to what
others want you to do
You must listen to yourself
Society
family
friends
do not know what
you must do
Only you know
and only you
can do what is
right for you
So start right now
You will need to
work very hard
You will need to
overcome many obstacles
You will need to go
against the better
judgment of many people
and you will need to
bypass their prejudices
But you can have
whatever you want
if you try hard enough
So start right now and
you will live a life
designed by you and
for you
and you will love
your life

— Susan Polis Schutz

Keep Looking Forward to the Future and to All You Might Be...

Don't let old mistakes or misfortunes hold you down: learn from them, forgive yourself — or others — and move on. Do not be bothered or discouraged by adversity. Instead, meet it as a challenge. Be empowered by the courage it takes you to overcome obstacles. Learn things. Learn something new every day.

Be interested in others and what they might teach you. But do not look for yourself in the faces of others. Do not look for who you are in other people's approval. As far as who you are and who you will become goes — the answer is always within yourself. Believe in yourself. Follow your heart and your dreams. You — like everyone else — will make mistakes. But as long as you are true to the strength within your own heart... you can never go wrong.

— Ashley Rice

You *Can* Do This

There isn't a person alive who
    doesn't want to make changes.
Every single person has something
    they can improve on.
Whether it's to give up a bad habit,
    make more money,
be physically fit,
    or any number of things,
there's always room to grow —
a way to become a better person.
Thousands of people consider
    making the effort,
yet there are few who successfully
    reach their goals.
You can be one of those few.

The power is within yourself;
it's in believing you can,
in knowing that you are the only one
who can change you.
You can begin at any moment,
regardless of past mistakes or failures.
The present and the future
are yours to live the way you want to.
Faith and discipline and
attitude and perception
are the keys to success.
Commit yourself, your time, and
your efforts
to allow the person you are...
to become the person
you want to be.

— Barbara Cage

The Sun Will Shine
on You Again

We all know that
no matter how many clouds
get in the way,
the sun keeps on shining.
No matter how many times its rays
are blocked from our view,
the sun will reappear on another day
to shine more brilliantly than before.
It takes determination
to outlast those dark clouds
that sometimes enter your life,
and patience to keep on shining
no matter what gets in your way.
But it all pays off eventually.
One of these days
when you least expect it,
you'll overcome your difficulties,
because you and the sun
have a lot in common:
You're both going to shine
no matter what.

— Barbara J. Hall

24 Things to Always Remember... and One Thing to Never Forget

Your presence is a present to the world.
You're unique and one of a kind.
Your life can be what you want it to be.
Take the days just one at a time.

Count your blessings, not your troubles.
You'll make it through whatever comes along.
Within you are so many answers.
Understand, have courage, be strong.

Don't put limits on yourself.
So many dreams are waiting to be realized.
Decisions are too important to leave to chance.
Reach for your peak, your goal, your prize.

Nothing wastes more energy than worrying.
The longer one carries a problem,
    the heavier it gets.
Don't take things too seriously.
Live a life of serenity, not a life of regrets.

Remember that a little love goes a long way.
Remember that a lot... goes forever.
Remember that friendship is a wise investment.
Life's treasures are people... together.

Realize that it's never too late.
Do ordinary things in an extraordinary way.
Have health and hope and happiness.
Take the time to wish upon a star.

And don't ever forget...
    for even a day... how very special you are.

— Collin McCarty

You'll Get Through This
One Day at a Time

If you keep on doing everything you can — a day at a time — you will get through this triumphantly.

Try not to worry. Try to look at what you're going through as a challenge rather than an obstacle, a time to develop patience. Have confidence in yourself, and realize that you can change your attitude even if you can't change the circumstances.

Look closely at your troubles. Don't let them cause you to give up. Befriend them and learn from them. Feel them lose their power over you. Allow them to teach you what you want to know and move on. Try not to be afraid.

You're a survivor. You're going to handle this. You're going to find strength you didn't know you had and grace to deal with whatever comes along. Pretty soon, you'll be on the other side, and it's just a matter of time until you will look back on this time in your life and draw strength from the knowledge that even though the road was rocky, you persevered and carried on.

— Donna Fargo

ACKNOWLEDGMENTS

The following is a partial list of authors whom the publisher especially wishes to thank for permission to reprint their works.

Nick Santana for "The First Step You Take...." Copyright © 1994 by Nick Santana. All rights reserved.

Deborah Weinberg for "You are beginning a personal journey...." Copyright © 1994 by Deborah Weinberg. All rights reserved.

Donna Newman for "Recovery Is a Learning Process" and "Sometimes admitting our weaknesses...." Copyright © 1994 by Donna Newman. All rights reserved.

Barbara J. Hall for "Don't Be Afraid to Talk About What You're Feeling." Copyright © 1994 by Barbara J. Hall. All rights reserved.

Parvene Michaels for "The Ghosts in Our Lives." Copyright © 1994 by Parvene Michaels. All rights reserved.

Tim Connor for "Detachment." Copyright © 1994 by Tim Connor. All rights reserved.

Portia Nelson for "Autobiography in Five Short Chapters." From There's a Hole in My Sidewalk. Copyright © 1992 by Portia Nelson. Published by Beyond Words Publishing, Inc., Hillsboro, Oregon. All rights reserved.

L. Dale Cox for "Peace Is Coming." Copyright © 1994 by L. Dale Cox. All rights reserved.

Sherée Heller for "I'm Finally Learning to Just Be 'Me'...." Copyright © 1994 by Sherée Heller. All rights reserved.

Marcy Perlmutter for "My Focus Is on Wellness." Copyright © 1994 by Marcy Perlmutter. All rights reserved.

Michele Rossi for "Be Hopeful... Think Positive." Copyright © 2002 by Michele Rossi. All rights reserved.

Dena Dilaconi for "Be True to Yourself, No Matter What." Copyright © 1994 by Dena Dilaconi. All rights reserved.

Lise Schlosser for "Beginning Today...." Copyright © 1994 by Lise Schlosser. All rights reserved.

Beth Fagan Quinn for "Have Faith...." Copyright © 1994 by Beth Fagan Quinn. All rights reserved.

Donna Levine Small for "What You Are Doing Takes Real Courage." Copyright © 1994 by Donna Levine Small. All rights reserved.

Linda E. Knight for "Stressful situations and trying times...." Copyright © 1994 by Linda E. Knight. All rights reserved.

Gail Mutterperl for "Be Kind to Yourself...." Copyright © 1994 by Gail Mutterperl. All rights reserved.

Barbara Cage for "You Can Do This." Copyright © 2002 by Barbara Cage. All rights reserved.

PrimaDonna Entertainment Corp. for "You'll Get Through This..." by Donna Fargo. Copyright © 2002 by PrimaDonna Entertainment Corp. All rights reserved.

A careful effort has been made to trace the ownership of poems used in this anthology in order to obtain permission to reprint copyrighted materials and give proper credit to the copyright owners. If any error or omission has occurred, it is completely inadvertent, and we would like to make corrections in future editions provided that written notification is made to the publisher:

SPS STUDIOS, INC., P.O. Box 4549, Boulder, Colorado 80306.